HOMEOWNER'S GUIDE TO
STRESS-FREE REMODELING

HOMEOWNER'S GUIDE TO STRESS-FREE REMODELING

Proven Strategies for a Successful Home Remodel from Start to Finish

Emma Auriemma-McKay

Emma Auriemma-McKay, Reno, Nevada
© 2019 by Emma Auriemma-McKay. All rights reserved.

ISBN-13: 978-0-578-44620-2 (paper)
ISBN-13: 978-0-578-44633-2 (.mobi)

Cover Art credit: Alexios Saskalidis, 187designz
Photo credit: Michelle Pheasant, Michelle Pheasant Design, Monterey,
CA   https://pheasantdesign.com/

CONTENTS

PREFACE

Remodeling is a new experience for most people, and like any new experience, it is best to be prepared for this new adventure, unlike I was for the first couple of remodels I did for resale.

Being an architect and drawing a project is quite different than being entrenched in it and being responsible for the finances, scheduling, and construction. When I did my first few personal remodels, I did everything wrong because I didn't prepare my budget properly, made too many improvements, and didn't have a good handle on construction time. In the end I didn't have a profitable project. As I have continued my practice and had more experience with the process, I have recognized what tools could be helpful for keeping the budget and time in check.

In my architectural practice, every one of my clients was totally new to building, and they found it overwhelming. As I developed hands-on tools to help them understand and follow the process in understandable language, the process went more smoothly. They were able to enjoy the journey with less anxiety and eventually have cherished memories of a gratifying experience while they celebrated and enjoyed their new homes.

The remodeling process takes expertise. You will be exposed to new terminology, new ways of thinking, new schedules, and for a while, a new way of living during construction. This book will help you get familiar with all these components, so you can stay in control, have confidence, and, most importantly, have fun during the progression of your project.

This book came about with support, encouragement, and valuable input from the following talented, award-winning, and well-published colleagues. I am forever grateful and thankful to each and every one of them.

Dan Fletcher, AIA
Principal, Fletcher Hardoin Architects, Monterey, CA
      www.http://fletcherhardoin.com

Matt McNickle, Licensed Contractor
Owner, McNickle Construction, Pacific Grove, CA
      jmattmcnickle@gmail.com
      https://sites.google.com/site/mcnickleconstruction

Kevin Heldt, Licensed Contractor
Owner, KDH Construction, Aptos, CA
      kdhconstruction.kh@gmail.com
      831-320-4566

Lee Harris, PE, LC, LEED AP
Owner, Light + Space an Architectural Lighting Firm, Reno, NV
      http://www.lightandspace.com

Wan Cone, AIA, LEED AP BD+C
Morris & Brown Architects, Reno, NV
      http://mbarenonv.com

Mercedes De La Garza, AIA
Principal, Mercedes de la Garza, Reno, NV and San Francisco, CA
      http://delagarzastudio.com

Philip Auchettl, CEO and David Lowenstein, COO
Principals, RAD LAB, San Diego, CA
      https://www.radlabsd.com/

Jack Hawkins, AIA, LEED
Principal, Hawkins and Associates, Reno, NV
      http://www.hawkinsarchitecture.com

Bill Fisher, AIA, LEED, GBCI
Principal, Fisher Architecture, Palmer Lake, CO
      http://www.fisharch.com

Elizabeth Metz
Owner, Elizabeth Metz Architect, Denver, CO
     https://www.emarchitect.com/philosophy

Joy Spatz, AIA, NCIDQ, LEED AP BD+C
Principal, Studio Collaborative, Denver, CO

    On the personal side, my ever-loving and supportive husband has cheered me on and let me devote most of my time to my new endeavors, and I am very appreciative of his support.

    I also want to mention my brilliant coach, Alina Vincent, who has guided me through the amazing journey of creating this book and *The Ultimate Stress-Free Home Remodeling Blueprint*, an online educational program that guides homeowners step-by-step through the home remodeling process.

    You can find the program directly at:

https://stressfreeremodeling.com/program

And join our *Stress-Free Remodeling Exchange* on Facebook at:

https://www.facebook.com/groups/1595182977178750

    Also, tune in and subscribe to our podcast *Stress-Free Remodeling*!

On iTunes: https://itunes.apple.com/us/podcast/stress-free-remodeling/id1438998766?mt=2

Or if you are not an iTunes user:
http://stressfreeremodeling.libsyn.com/

EMMA AURIEMMA-MCKAY

1

YOU ARE IN CONTROL

I'm going to share with you exactly how to line up professional, trustworthy people to work with and how to have a smooth home remodel (no matter how big or small). But before I can do that, you must ask yourself the following questions:

- Have you ever felt like your home remodel is going to cost way too much money or take too long to complete?

- Is there a part of you that's worried you won't actually get what you want because the architect or contractor will take over?

- Have you ever felt overwhelmed about the actual process and not sure where to start?

- Do you wish you could wave a magic wand and–poof–make your dream remodel magically appear?

Do any of these questions sound like you? If so, then this book is for you.

After reading this book, you will have the answers and the control to dissolve the above hesitations—except for the last one. I can do magic, but that wish is a little beyond my powers. Unfortunately, I don't have that kind of magic wand! However, I can promise you that you and your team will have a great journey together to achieve your dream.

The building industry has its own language and systems, as does every industry. If you have never been involved in a construction project, you will recognize words for things you know and words for things you don't know. Consider your remodel process like learning a new language. When I travel to a foreign country, I usually try to learn a few basic words. There are slang expressions that locals use and in that new language there is a new way of structuring a thought into a sentence. This is similar to you embarking on a building or remodeling project. Knowing some basics will help you be more comfortable, be a better communicator, and have an easier time navigating through the building phases. Knowledge will protect you from being taken advantage of, keep you in control, and enable you to have fun and enjoy the process—so consider this book as your translation manual.

Whatever your reason and whatever size remodel project you are thinking about, there is a proven step-by-step system every architect and design professional uses. The design and construction process is very involved. Without good guidance it may lead you to places you don't want to go: wrong decisions, running over budget, and ending up in a "forever" timeline. Whether you are doing a smaller project yourself or hiring an architect for a larger scale project, the information, decisions, and design steps will all be the same, but the cost and time factors will vary. Knowing the steps of the process, the time factors, all the pieces that need to be in place, and how all that fits and interacts together will give you amazing results. This book will help you become aware of potential circumstances and help you avoid getting into those situations.

When I began my practice, at first new clients stayed bewildered and confused about the process of their remodel, despite the orientation and overview I would describe. As a result, I began creating questionnaires for them to clarify their ideas and reference tools to give them an overall picture of the process and each phase along the way. Both were helpful to aid them in making informed decisions. Armed with the information my tools provided, my clients became great participants in their own projects, which helped move them along more quickly and smoothly–and they got exactly what they wanted!

Remodeling is an enormous undertaking. If it is your first time, it can be daunting not knowing where to begin—what you need, what to expect, how much it will cost, or who to get to help you.

Working with the right team and having the proper guidance will make your remodel experience one of the most exciting adventures of your life. This journey requires getting to know you and your family's intricacies in order to end up with a finished project that gives you pride, a sense of accomplishment, and not only increases the enjoyment value of your life but also the price value of your home.

This book presents five essential elements to be in control of your remodel:

- Have the knowledge and be prepared
- Do your research
- Have your budget
- Know your plan
- Have a first-rate team

In the following pages, there will be valuable insights and information that will enable you to talk the professional lingo and manage your project to keep it on time and budget.

QUESTIONS: YOU ARE IN CONTROL

1. What is your big dream vision?

2. Do you have a set budget?

3. Do you feel you understand the remodeling process?

4. What kind of support would be most helpful for you at this point?

5. What are the most important items you want to know about the remodeling process?

2

IS IT RIGHT FOR YOU NOW?

WHY NOW?

Your home may be continually needing repair work, or your family may have outgrown your present space. Your home may house older bathroom fixtures and kitchen appliances that can be energy and water hogs, increasing your monthly bills.

Upgrading or remodeling your home can increase its value exponentially. That in itself makes a compelling reason to invest in a change. Saving your sanity could be another compelling reason if you are living with daily frustrations such as waiting forever for someone to vacate the bathroom. If your home isn't an enjoyable place to live, your health and family relations are at risk.

GET PAID BACK

Adding even minor cosmetic items can increase the value of your home. Some of the simplest changes are—

- Replacing the front door

- Replacing the garage door

- Adding new siding or stucco

- Installing new shutters or a simple architectural element

These are only external cosmetic changes but will provide impressive curb appeal, which will spike the value of your home and give you a new fondness for it. You may recoup nearly the entire investment of cosmetic improvements like these when you sell your home. Don't forget landscaping either, which is an important feature for eye-catching curb appeal. Clean it up or add some vegetation that is enhancing and well planned.

More significant changes will greatly impact the value of your home as well as the quality of your life. The most popular remodeling projects are—

- Kitchen

- Bath

- Basement

- Deck

Up to 80% of your investment in these projects can be recouped in most areas of the country! When considering one of these redos, I suggest analyzing how that area now functions and what improvements can be made as well as considering how the area relates to the adjacent rooms and even your entire home. Reconfiguring an adjacent area in your redo may offer significantly more functionality. For example, your existing kitchen may have been located in the wrong place to begin with. If it is in the front of the house and you use the back deck very often but have to walk down a long hallway to get outside, consider changing the location of the kitchen in order to make the trip from the kitchen to where you serve and enjoy your meals shorter!

Here is an example of a real solution. As part of a much larger project, my client asked me to redesign the kitchen, which was in the back of his house, to accommodate a dining nook. When I asked the family how they used the house, they said they actually always migrated to the living room in the front of the house to have coffee, breakfast, and most meals, because the light and view were so much more enjoyable. As we evaluated their options, I suggested that we relocate the kitchen to the front of the house and added a nice deck for them to enjoy, which is what they chose to do. Now they enjoy their morning coffees and enjoy the view in their cozy new kitchen as the day comes alive and have their summer dinners conveniently on the adjacent covered porch as the day slips away to an end.

Why enhance an important part of your home—the heart of your home—if it doesn't function the way you want it to in the first place? Relocating a kitchen or bath may cause an increase in cost because plumbing and gas lines will need to be extended. However, having a new kitchen that you love and in a location that functions wonderfully may offset the additional expense to make it well worth it for your family.

Listed below are some of the possible additional costs associated with relocating appliances and fixtures.

Estimated Cost:	Description of Work:
$1,000 to $2,000	Relocate sinks and gas lines if you have a one-story house with a crawl space, depending on the new location's distance from the original location. If you have a multistory house, the price can go much higher, depending on the complexity and repair work that will need to be done.

$3.40-$5.70/linear ft.	Additional cost to cut through a 4" concrete slab to accommodate the new lines.
$6,000-$8,000	Relocate a sink and couple of appliances within an existing kitchen.

For preliminary planning, you can include these numbers in your budget, but to accurately estimate the cost for your specific project, you should get estimates from a couple of plumbers.

Looking at potential returns on your investment is exciting, but keep in mind the value of your home in relation to the value of other homes in your surrounding neighborhood. You don't want to over-invest so that the value of your home after the remodel will be far above the rest of your neighborhood. If this is your forever home, that can be fine, but if you are considering selling, you may not recoup your investment. Discover which remodeling projects can increase the value of your home in the "Highest Payback Remodeling Projects" report found at the link below:

https://s3-us-west-1.amazonaws.com/stressfreeremodeling/Payback.pdf

SOME COMPELLING REASONS TO REMODEL

1. You are wondering where to put the new baby.

2. A loved one has fallen ill, and you want to accommodate his or her special needs within your existing home while maintaining your privacy.

3. Your kids are in their teens, everyone needs more personal space, and the family needs more community space to enjoy activities together.

4. An in-law is moving in, and you will want them and your family to have their own space.

5. Someone needs a home office or hobby room.

6. Living with one bathroom for five people has grown tiresome, and you are dying for your master bathroom retreat.

7. Mother nature has pushed you into the decision to remodel by doing serious damage to your home, and now you have the opportunity to rebuild what you want.

8. You are tired of being cooped up in the kitchen missing all the fun because you are always cooking dinner when your guests arrive, and they are socializing without you.

9. You are thinking ahead about how to age in place when you are more mature, realizing you may need wider hallways and more spacious bathrooms to accommodate a wheelchair, or ramps, and handrails for safety.

10. You need more room than your existing home, but you have strong ties to your neighborhood, and schools and don't want to relocate.

11. You have purchased a new home but need to redesign it to your family's specific needs.

HOW REMODELING CAN CHANGE YOUR LIFE

Remodels are initiated for a variety of reasons, one being health reasons. For example, in one of my client's home, mold was detected that was causing him health problems. The area that had to be corrected was in the master bedroom where the client was considering removing a wall. Because rectifying the mold situation was covered by insurance, much of the extra work to eliminate the wall was paid for by the insurance. At the conclusion of the project, the client not only had his health restored, but also enjoyed a more spacious master bedroom. This is a small example of how an unfortunate situation can be transformed into a great advantage.

Another common reason to remodel is that a family may simply outgrow the space of their existing home. One family with two pre-teens decided their home was getting too congested. To accommodate their needs, they added a second story. This remodel gave them an additional family room where the pre-teens could entertain their friends in addition to their own bedroom. The parents also benefited with a private second floor master retreat and the dad got a home office. With the extra space, their lives flowed more smoothly, and they each valued their private space. They achieved this enhanced lifestyle by not being up-rooted but were able to stay in the neighborhood and enjoy the schools they loved.

BEFORE YOU REMODEL—ASSESS AND INVESTIGATE

It is very important to articulate and plan your project and budget. If you are planning your project on your own, there are tools that can help you. You must investigate and evaluate how the spaces in your home function now and how the function can be improved. If you are hiring an architect, he or she will guide you through this process.

The architect will interview you with numerous questions to understand and assess your family's particulars. Such questions may include the following:

- How is your household used?
- What activities does everyone like to do, and where do they like to do those activities?
- What are your needs and wants?
- How much space is required?
- What architectural styles do you prefer?
- What is your end goal for the remodel?

As you can see, there are many levels of questions to think about. You can have these preliminary answers prepared and doing so will help you identify what your remodel needs to provide before you meet with the architect.

This may sound trite, but another compelling reason to remodel is that not remodeling or doing the things that you have been dreaming about for years can cause emotional regret. Time is moving on, kids are growing up, and if you don't take action, you could miss out on enjoying and cherishing your home the way you have been envisioning.

QUESTIONS: IS IT RIGHT FOR YOU NOW?

1. What are the two top reasons why you want to remodel?
2. When you remodel, how will it change your life?
3. Is increasing the value of your home of interest or importance?
4. What payback or return on investment are you interested in?
5. Which areas will you consider remodeling?
6. What do you like the most about your home the way it is?
7. What would make it better?
8. What would be your biggest regret if you don't remodel now?

3

HOW TO GET MORE WITH LESS

DREAM THE POSSIBILITIES—THE SKY IS THE LIMIT

Don't start a project with blinders on. Sometimes people start a project so laser-focused on one thing that they miss realizing more potential for themselves. Dream the biggest dream possible, and then have a reality check about what can actually be accomplished. Your professional may very well provide a creative design, so you can have everything you want.

ENLIST THE CREATIVITY OF A PROFESSIONAL

While you may have an idea of what you want to do, I believe if you do not consult with a professional about your options, you could limit your project to only what you envision and know, thus, missing what could be great opportunities. Professional architects and certified interior designers have dealt with numerous kinds of situations and can offer solutions beyond your realm of experience and exposure. With their ingenuity and experience, they will be able to help evaluate whether your project can be expanded in a way that makes economical and emotional sense to give you more functionality.

Using the term "addition" doesn't always refer to additional square footage on to your home. You can have enhancing additions internally if the space of your floor plan is used efficiently. A professional may see the potential for achieving more than what you originally planned for about the same cost. Examples of additions that could significantly enhance your home for a small increase in a project's overall cost include accommodating a half bath, storage, or laundry room in an under-utilized area.

The following are a few examples of actual projects where, with creativity, I was able to give my clients far more than they expected.

Example One: Bathroom and Laundry Room Addition. One project I completed for a client started as a simple bathroom remodel. When I first explored the home with the client, we noticed an awkward unused hallway and a closet adjacent to the bathroom, so I proposed to reconfigure the spaces. In doing so, we captured added space for a spacious bathroom and a laundry room, neither of which were in the original plan—although they had been on the client's wish list.

Example Two: Luxurious Bathroom Expansion. Another project I completed was for a family who wanted to update the bathroom, kitchen, and a few other odds and ends. There were no existing drawings of the home, and during the process of doing the site survey and initial plans, we discovered a five-foot void between the bathroom and living room! We had hoped to find a hidden treasure when we opened up the wall, but there was only empty space. In a sense the treasure was to have the extra space to incorporate into the bathroom. With the additional space, they got a longer, more luxurious sink counter and cabinet and added an oversized shower area.

Example Three: Spacious Guest Room Expansion. Another project involved an addition to a living room. Before our project began, the existing living room was reached by four steps up from the main house, leaving a six-foot crawl space below. During the planning, the clients decided they wanted an additional guest room, but there wasn't room in the existing footprint of the home to accommodate one. The only potential space was the space under the existing living room and planned addition, but the clearance was only six feet-six inches. We decided to dig out under the new living room space to achieve a required eight-foot ceiling for the spacious guest room they desired.

Example Four: Maximized Charming Cottage View. A woman who was planning for her retirement home brought me one of the most interesting projects of my career. She had bought a charming cottage that had an expansive view of a bay. It was obvious the kitchen and bath needed remodeling, but after analyzing the entire floor plan, it was clear to both of us that the cottage's best feature, the view, could only be enjoyed from one of its rooms, while the other rooms had no view. I examined the plans and confirmed that the home's three central walls were not load bearing. In the new design plan, those three walls were removed, opening the space, and the full dramatic view of the bay could be enjoyed from the kitchen, living room, dining room, and sun porch.

The above are great examples of making the most of what you have with the help of a keen professional eye.

My colleague, architect Bill Fisher, whose Colorado Springs architecture firm proudly provides impressive, unique architectural design that serves his clients' function, budget, and aesthetics, assures: "There are always a variety of solutions. That is why it is to your advantage to work with a professional and allow their trained eyes and talent to design a project that provides the most functionality within the space you have."

Bill offers this advice for working with an architect: "Be open and flexible, and take time to truly consider their suggestions. Invariably, you will be surprised at how much their design solutions offer and what they can save you in cost at the same time."

Remodeling without an architect is risky, and it is also important to be flexible when enlisting your architect or designer for your team. Bill also suggests, "If your goal is to get more for less, don't approach an architect with your mind closed about possibilities and adjustments to your project." This can have unfortunate results, as he illustrates in the following example.

Bill told me about potential clients who came to him with a one-size-fits-all design plan they'd bought on the internet and were absolutely determined to use. After visiting the site, Bill realized that their plan took no consideration of the orientation, views, and other site amenities. When the clients were not willing to incorporate his suggestions to adjust the design into a more suitable solution—one which would have applied their financial and physical resources more responsibly and would have utilized their home site in a better way—he declined to do the project. Bill thought his integrity as an architect would be compromised if he provided a less-than-ideal solution for the client.

You will have a much more positive experience and outcome if, unlike Bill's potential clients, you stay open-minded and take advantage of your architect's suggestions. Remember they are aimed at achieving a beautiful and well-planned home for you.

I recommend that you interview architects and select someone whose opinion you respect and who will treat your needs thoughtfully as well. It is essential to get the architect on board early on so they can help you create great ideas. It's also a good idea to enlist a contractor in the early stages to help you keep your budget on track and perhaps give input on the building methodology.

A good time to bring an architect on board is before you begin looking to purchase a lot. Jack Hawkins, principal of Hawkins and Associates, a Reno, Nevada, architecture firm with a reputation for exceptional modern architecture and interiors, suggests that you "work with an architect as early as the selection of your building site, since they can evaluate a site more comprehensively. You may

consider a location ideal, but an architect can evaluate it on a variety
of levels to ensure that it can accommodate your vision."

QUESTIONS: HOW TO GET MORE WITH LESS

1.   Is there an area that is underused in your home?

2.   Is there an area in your home that needs more space? Can
     more space be captured from an adjacent, underused area,
     or will you need to build on a new addition?

3.   Is there an item on your wish list that can be incorporated
     into your new plan?

4.   Can you enhance existing areas with more light, more space,
     or higher ceilings?

4

NEW, UNEXPECTED WAYS TO SAVE

HEALTH SAVINGS ARE PRICELESS

Typical finishes used in homes and offices can contain toxic airborne particles known as volatile organic compounds (VOCs), which can be detrimental to the quality to your indoor environment.

If you walk into a newly remodeled home or office building and there is an unpleasant odor, you may be experiencing VOCs. As certain materials such as paint or carpet adhesives cure, their toxic particles are released into the indoor air, causing these odors. Breathing those toxins can cause allergic reactions such as sneezing, coughing, wheezing, running nose, and skin irritations. For example, a common ingredient for adhesives is formaldehyde. When airborne, formaldehyde particles can cause respiratory irritation, dizziness, and even nausea.

Studies show that continued exposure to these toxins can cause cancers. It is important to have good air circulation to maintain a healthy indoor air quality when you use these products. Keep in mind, however, that these particles can continue to be emitted up to a year after installation, and sometimes even longer. Sick Building Syndrome is the term for these reactions caused by buildings that have VOC-emitting finishes.

The good news is there are materials available that do not emit these toxins. If you have concerns about "healthy" or "green" building materials, look for VOC-free designations when shopping for finish materials such as furniture, carpet, cabinets, paint, and wall covering. The adhesives for carpet and wall covering can also be certified free of VOCs. Upholstery, drapery fabrics, and the structural components of furniture can also have these same afflictions. Inquire about the content of those materials and look for products that feature an Eco Label or similar indicating they are VOC-free.

Below is the link to the resource report, "Energy Conserving Products and Systems That Save You Money," for more information about organizations that monitor products to meet toxin-free standards and offer information about products and manufacturers:

https://s3-us-west-1.amazonaws.com/stressfreeremodeling/Energy.pdf

Savings using VOC-free products are subtle. They will not necessarily reduce your monthly statements but rather result in potential savings on health care and eliminate the need for a costly HVAC system to eliminate toxins in the air.

ABOUT THE ENERGY STAR® DESIGNATION

The Environmental Protection Agency, which administers the ENERGY STAR® program, describes it this way on the program's website:

"ENERGY STAR® is the government-backed symbol for energy efficiency, providing simple, credible, and unbiased information that consumers and businesses rely on to make well-informed decisions.

Thousands of industrial, commercial, utility, state, and loc organizations— including more than 40% of the Fortune 500®—rely on their partnership with the U.S. Environmental Protection Agency (EPA) to deliver cost-saving energy efficiency solutions. Ninety-percent of American households recognize the ENERGY STAR®, making it one of the most widely recognized consumer symbols in the nation. Together, since 1992, ENERGY STAR® and its partners have helped save American families and businesses more than $450 billion and over 3.5 trillion kilowatt-hours of electricity while also achieving broad emissions reductions—all through voluntary action."

Some products listed include appliances, HVAC equipment, office equipment, residential lighting, windows, doors, skylights, and even homes. Using these products can reduce energy costs by at least 30%!

You can reduce your taxes for the year if you purchase an ENERGY STAR® product. Energy tax credits are available by using the energy tax credit Form 5695.

EFFICIENT PRODUCTS, BUILDING METHODS, AND FIXTURES

Lighting Fixtures

ENERGY STAR®-rated appliances and lighting fixtures save energy. Lighting fixtures not only use less energy to run but also produce minimal heat, so you don't have unwanted heat gain causing extra cooling costs in warm weather. ENERGY STAR®-rated lamps and fixtures have much longer life spans, which will save on the cost of additional replacements. Fluorescent and LED lamps and bulbs have come a long way from when they first appeared on the market. Their light color now matches that of the warmth of incandescent lights and are available in a variety of warm and cool light spectrums. Many of these lamps and fixtures can also be dimmed.

Lee Harris, owner of Light +Space, an outstanding architectural lighting design firm in Reno, NV, shares, "Many new and modern lighting systems have the ability to conserve money and energy. For instance, programmable lighting systems allow you to set and choose different dimming scenes when the lights are turned on in a room, which can save energy. Using dimmed lighting levels with incandescent lamps will save as well, since their life is greatly increased when dimmed. Occupancy sensors can also save money in rooms where lights may be left on without being noticed, such as closets, storage areas, utility rooms, and bathrooms. There are also shut-off timers for bathroom exhaust fans."

Plumbing Products

Plumbing fixture manufacturers have responded by producing fixtures that conserve water by allowing less water flow. Low-flow toilets are available to save water. New technologies have been developed to flush with a fraction of the amount of water compared to older fixtures. Modern showerheads and faucets also are available with low flow features. Replacing older dishwashers and washing machines can also save energy and water. New models use newer technologies to do a good job using much lower amounts of water.

Below is a chart comparing older flow rates with flow rates of newer fixtures now available. Appliances, faucets, and showerhead flow rates are described in gallons per minute. Toilets are described in gallons per flush.

Fixture:	Modern, Low-flow:	Traditional:
Sink Faucets	1.5 gallons per minute	2.2-2.5 gallons per minute
Showerheads	< 2.0 gallons per minute	2.5 gallons per minute
Toilets	1.3 gallons per flush	3.5-7 gallons per flush
Dishwashers	4 Gallons per wash	13-18 gallons per wash
Washing Machines	13 gallons per wash	25 gallons per wash

Fenestration Products

Windows, doors, and skylights can also be ENERGY STAR®-rated, and they are tested and verified by the National Fenestration Rating Council (NFRC) to limit the amount of heat and cold that can seep through them into conditioned living spaces once they are installed properly. You may wish to choose windows and doors that utilize glass with a low E rating, usually provided by a special coating on the glass itself. An E rating means that the glass reflects both heat and light back to its source, helping your home stay cooler in the summer and warmer in the winter. It also helps protect against UV fading on any nearby furniture. For more information about window products and performance, the following reference report "Energy Conserving Products and Systems That Save You Money" is helpful:

https://s3-us-west-1.amazonaws.com/stressfreeremodeling/Energy.pdf

DESIGN AND CONSTRUCTION CONSIDERATIONS

Wood Construction

Typical wood construction materials consist of solid lumber, referred to as balloon framing and stick framing. The typical members are 2 in. x 4 in. and 2 in. x 6 in. wood studs for walls and wood joists for floors, 4 in. x 4 in. or 6 in. x 6 in. posts for beams as required, and 4 ft. x 8 ft. plywood sheathing panels. In the last few years, there has been much innovation in these basic building materials, and you may want to ask your architect and contractor about composites that provide higher strength capacities, insulation ratings, and fire-retardant properties.

The wood industry is continually experimenting and developing new materials. A twelve-story building can now be built out of wood! Structural members can be composed of composites, wood chips, dust, and resin. Depending on the building design, these options can save on material, cost, and construction time. If you are also interested in preserving the environment by conserving the natural resource of trees, products that use recycled wood and wood by-products can be specified into your project.

As wall framing members, standard 2 in. x 4 in. wood studs are limited to between 10 ft. and 14 ft. high, depending on the spacing and environmental factors for structural consideration, such as wind. The high ceilings that are desirable these days may require 2 in. x 6 in. wall studs. In addition, many newer homes use 2 in. x 6 in. wall studs so that a thicker, higher rated insulation can be used, which saves on heating and cooling costs. Using the wider studs a double advantage is gained, both for height and better insulation.

Soundproofing—Not Money-saving, but Sanity-saving

Consider soundproofing. If you have a laundry room, mechanical room, music, or media room next to a bedroom or office, noise can become an annoyance to occupants. Sound is vibration, and walls can include insulation to greatly minimize sound transference. Newer plywood panels also provide soundproofing characteristics, which can be great for walls or floors.

If you have a home office that needs to be quiet so that you appear to be working from a professional environment, or if you are doing recording work, you may consider sound insulating water pipes and heating systems for minimal sound distractions.

Framing And Ceiling Space

Roofing is framed in rafters or trusses. If you are considering a higher ceiling or open ceiling, you should start by deciding what you want it to look like. Here are a variety of options:

- A sloped ceiling following the roof line.
- Sloped ceiling edges from the walls into the room center, leading to a higher flat ceiling.
- Exposed beams in the sloping or flat ceiling.
- Flat ceiling with step-ups to give more height.

There are different ways to achieve an exposed beam look if that interests you. You can choose to expose the actual structural beams or hide the roof framing structure above the ceiling and add additional fake cosmetic beams. For example, if you want a sloped ceiling with exposed beams, the roof framing will be designed so that the exposed beams are the actual structural members. Having an open, sloped ceiling with exposed structural beams is dramatic; however, one drawback is that there will be no room in the ceiling for recessed lighting. To accommodate recessed lighting, the drywall will have to be framed down to create the required space from the roof sheeting and insulation to the ceiling finish to accommodate your selected recessed fixtures. Another option is to install track lighting.

Alternatively, the roof can be framed with rafters or wood trusses that are hidden above the finished ceiling. Then cosmetic fake beams can be installed at the finished ceiling to give the appearance of an exposed beam structure. Two advantages of the synthetic members are that they are lighter weight, and they have a hollow interior through which electrical wires and cables can be run. If your exposed beams are also structural members, the electrical will be coordinated differently. Lightweight, decorative beams may save construction costs by avoiding the need for extra framing or expensive track lighting.

Deciding what kind of ceiling you want involves numerous related decisions and coordination with the contractor, lighting consultant, engineer and architect. This is an example of how important is to plan ahead and understand all the implications one decision can have. For example, if you decided to have exposed beams that also serve as the structural framing for the roof and ceiling, but overlooked the need for adequate space to accommodate both the beams and the lighting fixtures, you would discover that framing down to accommodate the lighting fixtures will diminish the size of the beam you want to expose. To produce the result you originally envisioned would require additional modifications that would increase both material and labor costs.

This is why I stress to consult professionals to account for these conditions ahead of time. Your architect will help you evaluate the best and most cost-effective construction method for your situation to help you make the best decision.

Heating Methods

Typically, the majority of new homes use forced air-heating systems, in which heated air runs through ducts and enters each room through a vent. The temperature is controlled with a thermostat that can also be used for cooling. Some systems can be zoned so that you can heat or cool a space at certain times of the day when it is most used, so that the whole system isn't blasting away, wasting energy on spaces that are not being used.

Forced Air Systems

Forced air systems are economical, but there are drawbacks. As soon as the system is turned off, the space cools down or warms up. It is difficult to maintain the same temperature throughout a home, especially if one space is far from the main heat or cooling source. Because the air must travel a long distance through the ducts to the outer locations, the desired temperature can be lost. Insulating the heating ducts is crucial to maintaining optimal temperatures throughout a home while minimizing heat temperature loss.

Radiant Heating

Radiators are a type of radiant heating usually found in older homes throughout the US. The modern version is radiant floor heating. These systems use a resistance wire system run by electricity. A more economical version is run with a boiler or hot water heater that circulates hot water through tubes. In new construction, flexible tubes are installed on top of the subfloor and embedded in a concrete slab. In a remodel, the tubing can be placed under the subfloor. Most flooring finish materials can be placed on top but thick carpet padding will not allow the benefit of the radiant heat to rise through it. If you have a concrete slab floor, you may be limited to the electric-run system, which adds a minimal thickness to the original floor slab. Doors will have to be cut a bit shorter, and there will be special conditions at exterior doors and existing cabinet bases.

Overall, a radiant heating system is 30% more efficient than a forced air system, will heat a home more uniformly, keep the home at a more consistent temperature, and can also be zoned. Keep in mind that a separate cooling system will be required.

Windows

I once heard an eloquent definition of architecture as "the lens in which to frame, view and connect with nature." Windows provide a great connection with the outdoors, which results in a great sense of tranquility. Scientific studies have proven that being in—or having a sense of being in—nature increases productivity, calmness, and a sense of well-being. Fortunately, today you have many more ways to include views of the outdoors in your planning. Windows are no longer confined to the 2 ft. x 3 ft. double-hung traditional option. Expansive glass areas can also be moveable, such as those provided by the Nana Wall Company at www.nanawall.com. An entire wall can become operable by folding or sliding members.

Depending on the style and design you want to achieve, you should consider the finishes of the window frames, whether wood, metal, or painted. The style can also be enhanced by the window configuration, size, and shape.

As discussed above, glass characteristics can provide UV protection, insulation, glare protection, and great strength. If you replace the single-pane windows in an average 3,000 square foot home with ENERGY STAR®-rated single-pane windows, a yearly savings of $126 - $465 can be realized. Double- and triple-paned glass windows also provide the additional efficiency of good insulation. By replacing existing double-pane windows with ENERGY STAR®-rated windows, a savings of $27 to $111 a year can be realized.

All these new alternatives may be your choice, but in some jurisdictions, they may also be requirements, especially regarding water-saving and energy-saving devices. The initial cost for some of these items may be a bit higher than the standard choice, but in the long run they will save money and even pay for themselves by reducing your utility bills.

As a summary, the chart below shows potential savings if various energy- and water-efficient products are used in a typical 2,500 square foot home. Total energy and water savings chart

Product:	Annual Savings:
Toilets, $19.20 each x 2	$ 40
HVAC	$1,400
Dishwasher (energy)	$ 35
Dishwasher (water)	$ 40
Refrigerator	$ 270
Windows $126-$465 (average)	$ 300
Lighting	$ 30
Clothes Dryer (energy)	$ 20
Radiant Heating (estimated)	$ 400
Total Potential Yearly Savings:	$2,535

As you see, making typical efficiency upgrades as discussed in this chapter could result in about $2,500 per year in energy and water bill savings for an average 2,500 square foot home.

Finally, using some of these energy-saving methods may allow you to save on your taxes.

The "Opportunities for Tax Credits from Your Remodel" report contains further information regarding potential tax credits, rebates, and financing for purchasing particular systems. Find the report at the link below:

https://s3-us-west-1.amazonaws.com/stressfreeremodeling/Tax.pdf

QUESTIONS: NEW AND EXCITING WAYS TO SAVE

1. What methods of savings are of most interest to you?

2. What old products are in your home that can be upgraded to newer money saving versions?

3. What methods do you intend to incorporate into your remodel?

5

ASSEMBLE YOUR PLAYERS

Planning a remodel or building project is similar to writing and producing a play. Remodeling your home will be one of the greatest productions of your life. Just as you would for a theatrical production, you will do extensive research and planning and look for the most interesting stories, and the best set designers, costume designers, crew, and performers. Similarly, much interviewing, coordinating, and planning are required to have a successful home remodel project. When you begin to plan your remodel, it will involve some reflective self-inquiry about your family, about your lifestyle, the kind of environment you want to create, how it will feel and function, and how you can save on operating costs by making informed and efficient choices. Planning well will ensure the project runs as smoothly as possible.

Like a playwright, you must first decide what roles are required for your project before you assess which players you want to hire in those roles. Arranging your remodeling team is similar to casting for a stage theater production. You have to know the script (your detailed remodeling plan), the actors (your contractors and subcontractors) and the roles (who will be responsible for which phases of work). A playwright puts together all the players and acts in a play to make the play a success. To relate this concept to your home remodel project, think of yourself as the playwright of your remodel: knowing your plan, the phases, and the required roles will result in a successful project.

A REMODEL'S CAST OF CHARACTERS

Here is the cast of players that will be involved in your remodel.

The Directors (You, the Owners)

You will cast your lead players, namely the architect and contractor. You will be responsible for having a clear idea of what you want to do, how it will function, and what it will look like. You will establish a budget. You will communicate this information to the architect, who will use it to determine the design direction of the project. You will also be responsible for payment to the architect and contractor to keep the project running.

The Playwright (You and Your Design Team)

Depending on the size of your project, you may choose to design it yourself. Even so, I urge you to have at least one consultation with an architect or interior designer to be assured you are maximizing your dollars and the potential and function of your remodel area. Again, because of their experience and training, professionals may recognize design potential and opportunities you are not aware of and may have suggestions for saving money.

Heroic Lead Character
(the Architect)

You and the architect will have a great rapport, sharing information and creating your project. The architect will interpret your information and create drawings of the plans that are required for your permit and construction. If there are other technical services required for your project, such as soils reports, energy calculations, structural engineering and so on, he or she will suggest and orchestrate reliable companies (supporting characters) for your project who have produced good work on previous projects. The architect will coordinate each company's expertise and information and incorporate that information into your construction documents in addition to escorting your project through approval and permit processes with your city's officials and procedures. He or she will also observe construction to ensure things are built according to the plans and assist in the final completion process.

As the client, you need to decide how much you want to be involved in the process alongside the architect. You may just want to write checks and have the keys handed to you, or you may want to roll up your sleeves and get totally immersed. Either way, you have the following important roles and responsibilities:

- Have a clear idea of what you want
- Have your finances in order
- Know your budget
- Make material and product decisions on time
- Make payments on time

Selecting an architect who is well suited for your project is similar to selecting a typecast actor for a particular role in a play. Some actors are known for comedy, some for scary thrillers, and some for western cowboy roles. Two examples of typecasting are Sean Connery in a spy role or John Wayne in a cowboy role.

Architects may be typecast in a sense, too. Jack Hawkins suggests an interesting notion: "Each architect has different strengths. One architect may have strengths in design, while another's strength may be engineering aspects of the building. Keeping the objectives of your project in mind when evaluating the specific strengths of different potential architects will help you formulate your questions and discussions with them, and ultimately help you make your final selection."

Sidekick or Second Lead Character (the Contractor)

The contractor hires the sub-contractors (more supporting characters) for the various work tasks on your project, such as concrete foundation, framing, electrical, roofing, tile work and so on. He or she schedules each trade's work in proper sequence for construction, orders project materials, and takes care of inspections with the city officials as required. It is the contractor's responsibility to keep the job on time and budget, building your dream into reality.

Supporting Characters
(Individual or Sub-contractors)

You, the architect, and the (general) contractor are the main characters in your play, but here are other numerous supporting actors who may be included as follows:

- Technical professionals or specialty consultants required (such as for lighting, energy, soils, and structural requirements) in order to help create the architect's construction documents.

- Sub-contractors for various trade work such as tile, painting, electrical, HVAC, plumbing, framing, roofing, flooring, carpet installers, etc.

- City Inspectors who conduct inspections and approvals throughout the project so your remodel can proceed.

- Inspectors from your lenders who ensure milestones are met in order to release funds.

- Home inspectors who perform initial inspections to confirm the existing building's conditions.

Each one of these characters has their script and must be scheduled to appear at the perfect time.

Typecasting for individual contractors has some of the same considerations as those for typecasting your architect. Keeping your project's objectives in mind, consider the different kinds of contractors available and their individual strengths as you interview and select your supporting cast as well.

You will need to decide what level of quality you require for each phase of your project. If you are doing a basic remodel without a lot of detail and specialty items, you don't need to hire a contractor who specializes in custom work. These kinds of contractors takes great pride in their work, love to spend time on details, and will be meticulous about the finished product. They will want to do a great job for you and want your project to be an impressive statement about them. Of course, this will be reflected in the time it takes to complete the project as well as the cost, and you may end up with a more expensive and lengthy project than you require.

On the other hand, if you intend to include lot of detail and specialty work, you don't want a contractor who will simply "just get the job done." They most likely will not have the sensitivity, resources, or concern for subtleties and precision such specialty work requires.

On the subject of typecasting: also be aware that your architect may typecast you as a client, evaluating whether you will be a good fit as a client. But you get to choose what "type" you will be. Will you be the diligent one who is prepared, makes timely decisions, and has great rapport with your professionals? The goal is to be working in a situation that is win-win for everyone, in which all parties are a good compatible fit with each other.

About Playing the General Contractor (Being Playwright, Director, and Lead)

You can choose to act as the general contractor for your remodel and be a "solo show," so to speak, playing the director, lead actors, and multiple other roles in your project. If that will be the case, be prepared and confident about the numerous levels of information you will be required to direct. The following are just some of the responsibilities of a general contractor:

- Hire the required sub-contractors.
- Organize the critical sequence of the trades for the construction process.
- Verify quality work of each trade and that of your own.
- Confirm that contracts with subcontractors are in order.
- Schedule inspections.
- Order the correct materials and correct amounts of materials.
- Keep tabs on the budget and time.
- Take the project through the building permit process.
- Be responsible for all the project liabilities.

When it comes to construction and remodeling, being a jack-of-all-trades is a time-consuming undertaking. Appraise what you are willing, skilled, and able to do on your project, and decide if you need to hire specialists for certain tasks. Note that laws often require some trade work to be done by a licensed contractor. During construction, there are numerous questions that arise daily that need to be resolved quickly. Some decisions may have consequences to other parts of the remodel, and this can have expensive and serious implications if the entirety of the project is not fully understood by the decision-maker. This is a major reason to consider hiring professional help.

An extreme version of being a remodeling "solo show" is to act not only as general contractor (playwright, director, and lead actor) but also to do all the work of the sub-contractors (supporting characters) on your project. This could mean that you plan to do all the designing, decision-making, planning, supervising, and performing the manual labor yourself without any hired labor at all, such as handling the saw and hammer and city hall yourself. If you choose this route, please keep in mind you must have licensed trade work as proper inspections as required.

You may desire to personally be in charge of a "solo" remodel project for the love of building, or you may want to save money. However, you should carefully evaluate how much time you will need to invest daily in order to adequately supervise a construction project, and the length of the time the project will take if you manage it in your free time versus hiring a general contractor who will oversee your project and commit the appropriate time and effort. The cost of hiring a "director" could be easily offset by a faster completion and fewer costly mistakes.

QUESTIONS: ASSEMBLE YOUR PLAYERS

1. How would you like to be typecast in your remodel?

2. Are you prepared and confident about the players your remodel will require?

3. Do you have the skills and resources available to manage your remodel?

6

HOW TO COMMUNICATE SO THAT YOU GET WHAT YOU WANT

To have your project go the way you want, take charge from the start. To do so, be informed about the remodeling process, know your budget, and have your information and documents gathered.

Philip Auchettl and David Loewenstein of RAD LAB Architecture in San Diego, California, are of the opinion that "being informed about the remodeling process will make you more comfortable with decision-making, more able to participate and work quickly through each phase, and allow the entire project to move more swiftly and smoothly." Their firm pioneers innovative architecture nationally and internationally and has been creating a buzz of excitement for their community projects.

Preparing for Your First Meeting

Here are five things you can do to prepare before you talk to an architect:

1. Research what you want to do and know your property.

2. Know your budget and financing.

3. Organize your required documents and information.

4. Hire the right kind of design professionals.

5. Understand the timeline for your project.

In order for an architect and contractor to do what you want, you must first be clear on your ideas, goals, and budget.

If you will be designing and contracting your project yourself, you don't have to convey your ideas to anyone, but it is still critical to have a very clear idea of what you are going to do. Otherwise, your project can change like the wind, cost more, take longer, and be physically and aesthetically uncoordinated. Especially if you feel as though you don't have a creative aptitude or don't have a clear idea of what you want, it is best to hire a professional to work with you on your design.

1. RESEARCH WHAT YOU WANT TO DO, AND KNOW YOUR PROPERTY

The first thing you must do is to know your home and your property. Make a list of requirements, priority items, and what you want to achieve—in both physical requirements and intangible requirements.

Examples may include the following:

- What you like about your existing home.

- Particular views you want to feature.

- Activity areas you want in the shade.

- Areas you want to be totally private from the street.

- The style you want to be prevalent.

Not only should you know the property you are planning to remodel, you should also conduct research at your city's building department to learn of any restrictions. This can save you from time spent dreaming up a great scheme that is legally impossible. Finding out about restrictions on your property early can deter you from remodeling and motivate you to relocate instead.

Only once you have done these evaluations can you develop a clear idea of how to move forward. This is important, so you can communicate this information to your architect. The more details you have, the better you can guide your architect. They will have a better understanding of how to synthesize your physical requirements and budget to the site conditions in order to achieve a stellar design for you.

Written information is important, but visuals are also a great aid to help the architect and contractor understand the style, design, and finishes you have in mind. There are numerous publications and online resources for images for this purpose. An architect and contractor can respond immediately to images you select and determine if your ideas and budget are in alignment. This brings me to the next subject: your budget and finances.

2. KNOW YOUR BUDGET AND FINANCING

Securing your financing is a major factor that goes hand in hand with step one. If you don't know your budget, you cannot direct your architect to keep within that parameter.

It's similar to the dilemma of which should come first, the chicken or the egg. If you have a certain amount of money set aside for your project, there is no guesswork; you know your budget. If you are applying for financing, the amount the bank will lend you may determine your budget. Either way, knowing your budget is a critical parameter to share with your architect right up front. Don't wait until all the drawings of your dream home are done and then suffer from sticker shock when the bids come in. An architect and contractor who are skilled at bringing projects in on budget can use their creativity to design and build a remodel that matches, and even exceeds, your vision.

Mercedes de la Garza, whose Reno, Nevada, architectural firm has received international recognition for her beautiful distinctive designs, advises: "You can't tell your architect what to do if you don't know your budget. Research and understand the costs per square foot attached to your design ideas and finishes and how they translate into the cost for your entire project. Realize also that the cost of construction varies from city to city, so it's important to know what your area's costs are." Like most architects, Mercedes is emphatic about the importance of knowing this information before she starts a project.

You may be thrilled with the amount you have to spend on your project. However, once you establish that amount, there are numerous additional costs besides construction that have to be accounted for. Examples are permit fees, architectural fees, and contractor profits. You'll need to work backwards to account for these costs. After subtracting these amounts from the total budget you have set, the remaining sum represents your actual project construction budget.

Do research on building costs to be assured your ideas and budget represent a viable project. Presenting ideas that represent a budget way over what you intend to spend will not help your architect understand what you are aiming for and may prevent them from creating a realistic plan.

3. ORGANIZE YOUR REQUIRED DOCUMENTS AND INFORMATION

As you do the research on the property, collect and copy the pertinent information to save for your records and to share with the architect.

One especially important item to locate or acquire is a set of construction documents or "as-builts," which detail your existing structures. "As-builts" are the architectural and engineering drawings from which your home was permitted and built. Typically, they show the site plan, floor plans, elevations, structure, and some building material specifications. Since drawings of the existing plan are what the new design will be based, your architect will require these. If you can find an existing set, it will save you the time and expense of having to engage a professional survey company to produce them. It will also be a great head start to have these documents gathered, and you will certainly impress the socks off your architect.

Do you need permits?

Cosmetic work such as painting, wall covering, cabinetry, and carpet or tile installation do not need permits, but moving walls, plumbing and electrical work do. I urge you to comply with this requirement because it is protection for you to ensure the work is done properly and to code. If you fail to obtain the necessary permits, not only are you risking unsafe construction in your home, but you also can incur penalties, and the work could be red-flagged by the building department who could force all work to stop until it is proven to be code-compliant. Such delays would cause an increase in construction time and costly fines. Like most construction and design professionals, I have heard of instances when a built structure was not properly permitted, and a city demanded it be torn down. In short, if the work isn't done properly, there can be problems and damages that can cost considerably more than the permit.

4. HIRE THE RIGHT KIND OF DESIGN PROFESSIONALS

The following are suggestions about the best design and architectural professionals to hire for your project. As I have said multiple times, even if you are designing and installing a project on your own, I would recommend having at least one consult with one of the following specialty professionals.

About Architects

If you have a project that involves rearranging much of the space of your home or your project needs coordination with other specialty professionals, you will want to hire an architect for the best results, protection, guidance, and strategy throughout all phases of your project. They are your advocates to help you navigate through the entirety of the project from beginning to end. Architects provide the biggest impact in the initial design phase, and there are situations that can require an architect to implement special design, technical, and political strategies in order to have your project be approved and be a success. An architect's expertise and overall understanding can save you significant money.

You interview and hire architects for their expertise. Even though you will be directing them as to your desires and requirements, they will be guiding you as to what they require from you and what each step of the process will be. You are a team and will be working together for the end goal of your beautiful home.

Typically, a bachelor's degree in architecture requires a minimum of five years of study. After receiving the degree, a lengthy internship must be logged before taking comprehensive licensing exams that cover legalities, building methods, structural methods, design, and ethics. Many architects belong to the professional organization called the American Institute of Architects (the AIA). The AIA has specific criteria for a licensed architect to become a member. Belonging to this organization is not a requirement to practice architecture, nor does it necessarily indicate the quality of an architect's work; however, members have access to exclusive educational programs and professional resources.

Architects are masters of—

- Designing and translating your vision to reality.

- Building methods and keeping the project within budget and codes.

- Coordinating with other specialists required for the project.

- Strategizing the project through design, planning, and permit approval.
- Assisting and coordinating through construction and completion.

Having all these attributes make an architect an invaluable asset to have on your team.

More Specifics about the Architect and Some Insider Secrets

"What the architect would like you to understand and know," explains architect Dan Fletcher, a long-time colleague of mine and a partner in Fletcher+Hardoin, an architectural firm in Monterey, California sought out for it's exquisite and elegant design solutions, "is that architects can solve a design problem based on your desires, needs, and budget, the site's constraints, and what is most likely to be approved. It should be a collaborative process between you and your architect, to put all the pieces together in an organized manner, so all the elements fit seamlessly together in the final design, from the big picture to the minute details."

Dan adds, "As you meet and interview different architects, be aware that they also are evaluating whether you and your project would be a good fit for them." In addition to discussing their firm and practice, architects also will ask what ideas you have for your project. They will want to know if you have done a building project before. If you haven't, you can share how you have become more informed about the process, including researching your property, learning about the process through reading this book, exploring other resources, or taking an online course such as *The Ultimate Stress-Free Home Remodeling Blueprint*. Building and construction has its own specific language, and taking some time to become familiar with it will make it easier for you to communicate and navigate through the process.

If you have done your homework, architects will see that you are familiar with the process. Have your notes and images ready to share with them. Be articulate and definitive about your intentions. If you have too many confusing or conflicting ideas, they may interpret these behaviors as signs that you will be an indecisive client who will require excessive time to get through the project. If you are prepared to present your thoughts as well as listen to your prospective architect's ideas, you will be starting this relationship in the best possible manner.

Elizabeth Metz, a well-noted architect from Denver, Colorado, whose stunning work is created by keeping the sculptural aspect of architecture in mind, states, "Once you have selected your architect, remember that his or her primary skill set is their experience and design ability, so allow them to exercise their creativity for a fabulous project. Architects are expert problem-solvers, and if you are open to their ideas and consider them carefully, you may find that the architect's design solutions are the best for your criteria and property."

Everyone has a role to play, and it should be clear from the beginning what those roles are. The architect needs your input and ideas. Within the standard design process, each architect has his or her own way to bring your project to fruition. Honor that and allow that freedom. Architects will also be guiding you, preparing you and advising you every step of the way. They will want to have a great rapport with you, and your questions are important to them. Asking questions is necessary, but be mindful that, beyond a certain point, micromanaging your architect will make him or her ineffective and unproductive. This often translates into delays, extra costs, and frustrations for all parties.

Architects have a gift for visualizing two-dimensional drawings as they build three-dimensional space in their brain. As an aid to people without that ability, most firms offer three-dimensional computer renderings or animations to facilitate collaboration and understanding through the design phase and to help you see and understand your end result.

Keep in mind that if the architect isn't producing a design that meets your vision, needs, and requirements, you may terminate your agreement. The standard AIA Owner and Architect Agreement includes a section for termination or suspension, and you should ensure that the contract you sign includes such a statement. That section will state how you should communicate an intention not to move forward with the architect and the project. It is common for the contract to require that the architect be paid for the work they have completed and expenses they have incurred, up to the date of termination. On the contrary, if a client is not performing properly, not paying invoices in a timely manner, not supplying them with requested information, etc., this section will also give the architect the option to terminate the agreement. I have done it, and I know others have as well. There may be other reasons for not continuing a project, for example, a death of a spouse, a financial situation, or a site situation. The same process will be required.

About Residential Designers

Some states have a professional licensing classification for residential designers. They have some training in both design and construction but not to the full extent of an architect. They are licensed only as a residential designer, not an architect, and have limitations on the scale of work and building type they are qualified to produce.

If you have design ideas for a small project, residential designers can assist you with designs both for the interior and the exterior, but the creativity and sensitivity required for this important design phase most likely is not their strength. They can prepare construction documents and take the documents through the permit process. The industry refers to drawings produced by a residential designer as a builder's set. These drawings include minimal details, compared to what an architect would provide, and will only specify generic finishes and broad building systems information, such as heating, cooling, and electrical. This lack of detailed information can lead to wide interpretation by the individual contractors bidding on your project. You will have to determine what degree of detailed specifications your residential designer will provide, what you are willing to research on your own, and what you will delegate to your contractor. A residential designer may also be hired to observe construction so that your project plans are built according to the plans.

About Interior Designers

Interior designers are qualified to do space planning of a project. An interior designer will either have a college degree or have accomplished a specialized training program. A designer holding an NCIDQ qualification (National Certificate of Interior Design Qualification) indicates a higher level of qualification. They have met a required level of education and training and have passed a professional exam. Interior designers are versed in finishes, fabrics, and furniture, and can assist coordinating all the design elements. They are familiar with building materials and can propose structural alterations but cannot provide engineering or drawings for the proposed structure. Some designers and decorators may have a particular style in which they like to design. Look at their previous work to ensure their design approach is what you have in mind.

If you are planning custom detailing such as built in cabinetry, special tile designs, or other special features, you might consider hiring an interior designer, for example, if your architect doesn't offer interior coordination because detail work is not his or her forte or interest. Interior designers can work closely with the architect to coordinate the special design elements. They will coordinate furniture arrangements, window coverings, and other elements that interface with the architecture. An important contribution of interior designers is that they can provide an overall harmonious design.

About Draftspersons and Computer Operators

If you are planning a small project such as removing one wall to expand a kitchen area and need drawings of the floor plan for permit and construction, a draftsperson/CAD draftsperson can draw them up for you. You tell them what to draw and they draw it up. Depending on your situation, for example, if the wall being removed is structural, the draftsperson will have to coordinate with a structural engineer to include the structural information to submit for the permit. Typically a draftsperson will not get involved in the permit process. That will be your responsibility.

If you are planning a more complex or larger project where you are moving multiple walls or building an addition to your existing home that involves engineering and other consultants, again, I urge you to get an architect or interior designer's input on the plans in the preliminary design stage to guarantee the best design.

While a draftsperson or computer operator may have the ability to draw up a set of plans and basic details, he or she may not have the skill to truly coordinate and understand all the required elements. In my experience, initially you may save money, but your plans may be insufficient. As a result, there may be items that will need to be added during construction or particular items not specified, such as windows, which can cause unplanned cost increases and delays in the construction schedule.

The following example will prove my point. My architect friend has designed a brand-new home that will be built by a local builder for herself and her husband. The builder's draftsperson/CAD operator is drawing up her plans, and she is finding inconsistencies and lack of coordination of key elements in his drawings. Being an architect, she can catch these incongruities and mistakes and correct them before construction begins. However, as a layperson, you may not have the knowledge to do so and can run into difficulties during construction.

About Decorators

A decorator will help you choose cosmetic improvements, wall colors, draperies, fabrics, furniture, and accessories. Keep in mind that a talented decorator may be self-taught and have little professional education because there are no certification requirements other than a business license.

About General Contractors

Unlike everyone else described in this section, general contractors are not part of your design team. "You hire a contractor to build your home project, not to design it," reminds architect Bill Fisher: "Many people call a contractor before they have considered an architect, because they don't realize they need a plan or don't understand that a contractor doesn't provide design."

Contractors do a great job of bringing the architect's drawings to life, and if you choose to hire a general contractor, they will be in charge of hiring and supervising the subcontractors, ordering materials, arranging inspections and taking on the liability for the project.

As part of the process to select a contractor, you will invite potential contractors to bid on your project. Collect three to five names to consider and interview them to get familiar with their approaches and personalities. Narrow down to at least three contractors before you request bids and compare their proposals.

Your architect can help you with your search for a contractor, suggesting reputable contractors with whom he or she has worked before and whose demeanor and quality of work are satisfactory. Alternatively, someone you know may have had a good experience with a contractor with whom you would like to work on your project. It still is a good idea to do due diligence and make background inquiries about any contractor you are considering. In order to feel secure that the candidate you are considering is trustworthy and has a good track record of keeping on time and budget, ask him or her for former clients' contact information and take the time to speak with those clients about their experience and working relationship. Also, you should check on the contractor's license status and credit standing. The license can be verified by calling your state's contractors licensing board. To check credit standing, ask the contractor who his or her regular suppliers are. You can follow up with those suppliers to be sure accounts are in good standing.

Receiving the bids can be confusing since each contractor has their own preparation format. What I have done in the past is made a spreadsheet with each category of contractor and plugged in their numbers for comparison. I also double check to ensure that all tasks have been included in each bid. On one occasion this spreadsheet really saved me, because one contractor had not accounted for the tile work, one left out hardware, and one left out site cleanup. This is an example of how honest mistakes can be made by anyone: these bids were from contractors with whom I had worked before and whom I trusted and respected.

You will have a few conversations with contractors to clarify what their numbers represent since some categories can be represented with a lump sum, such as tile work or demolition. For example, one contractor may break out the tile work into material and labor, while another contractor will include both in a lump sum. You will want to have the second contractor break his numbers down in the same fashion to get a true price comparison. Another question would be how each contractor will account for demolition and removal. The numbers for each item will vary a bit, but if there are huge discrepancies between bids, talk to the particular contractors for clarification. Ideally, if all the contractors use one format, your exercise in comparing bids will be much easier and faster.

It is tempting to choose the contractor with the lowest bid, but typically the lowest bidder is not the best hire. As you do your due diligence as suggested above and feel comfortable the contractor is compatible with your project and your personality, you will feel secure in your final selection.

Matt McNichol, a highly-regarded, first-rate general contractor and long-time friend in Monterey, California, strongly suggests, "Talk to the contractor's former clients and tour a few projects, so you can witness the quality of their work in person and have former clients confirm their performance. You should feel comfortable that a contractor's personality is compatible with yours and trust the quality of his work, so that you will not worry throughout the project."

It is also a good practice to have contractors involved in the early stages of your project because they can assist with keeping the budget in line and offering ideas about building techniques to the architect to help save time and money.

Kevin Heldt from the San Francisco Bay area is another well sought after and highly-esteemed general contractor with whom I have worked on some challenging projects, says, "The contractor is also your advocate. They protect you from unworthy subcontractors and inferior work. Working with a contractor will get you the best tradesmen for the best prices. This alone justifies their well-deserved markups."

If you are able to obtain plans for your project without an architect's assistance, and you choose to hire only a contractor without the support of an architect, then you will be in the lead role, managing the project along with the contractor. Request timelines, payment schedules, and progress reports from the contractor before work begins. Be sure the proper permits are obtained, your home insurance is in order, and your contract with the contractor is in order. The permit process has various requirements for scheduling, fees, etc. Securing a permit and proper inspections gives you protection that the project complies with codes and is constructed properly. Remember, should you be discovered doing work without a permit, there are heavy consequences in the form of fines, project delays, and the possible demolition of your completed work in order to meet code requirements.

Jack Hawkins notes, "During the construction process there will be decisions that result in changes and the use of alternative building methods. One decision can have effects on a variety of other areas of your project—effects that neither you nor your contractor may anticipate. To avoid such surprises, it is invaluable to keep an architect involved during the construction who understands the ramifications of each decision. They can save you from making mistakes which translate into additional costs and time."

Everyone is always worried about the job running over the deadline. Be prepared to be flexible and extend your deadline for a variety of challenges that might come up during your project. Examples of things that may cause delays over which your contractor has little or no control include weather conditions and incorrect delivered supplies. You can also offer incentives to the contractor to motivate him or her to finish on time even in the face of challenges.

If you have a certain building talent, such as painting, that you would like to contribute to your project, either for fun or to save money, you can consult with your contractor and he or she will arrange a particular time in the schedule for you to perform that task.

5. UNDERSTAND THE TIMELINE

You may require that your project be completed at a specific time. For example—

- Your son may be getting married, and you offered to host the wedding in your new home.

- You want the kitchen and dining room completed for a huge family gathering on a particular holiday.

If you have this kind time constraint, consult an architect and contractor immediately to ensure your deadlines can realistically be meet. They will be honest and realistic, and you should honor truthfulness if it cannot be done. Your desire to complete on a certain date does not mean it will happen unless there is a generous amount of time allotted. Every project is begun with the intention of finishing by the initial estimated date, but even obstacles as simple as weather conditions can cause delays and prevent your project from meeting your deadline.

There are various phases of a remodel project, and understanding what takes place and the normal time required for each particular phase is important. Your architect will explain each phase, but there are some processes over which he or she has no control. For example, you may be required to have a Planning Commission or other agency review and approve your plans before submitting for permit. It is possible that they will not approve an aspect of your project. The architect will have to revise the drawings, resubmit them, and reschedule another meeting for the next review. This process can delay a project's construction start for months. Researching your property thoroughly at the building department as suggested in the beginning of this section may provide clues to potential items that could be denied, and help you avoid these delays.

The bottom line is *patience, patience, and patience.*

"There will be times when you may think nothing is going on, but I can assure you the architect is putting great effort into your project, coordinating with various consultants and corresponding with various agencies," stresses Joy Spatz, architect and owner of Studio Collaborative, a well-respected Denver, Colorado, architectural firm. "After you have interacted with the architect in the beginning of the design process, and once you review and sign off on the design drawings, you won't be involved very much. Your most important involvement will be to keep the finances flowing to keep the work progressing. This means paying on time."

Once the plans are submitted to your city's building department for the plan check process to obtain your permit, it can be a long game of waiting if you are in a jurisdiction that is busy. Again, *patience, patience, patience.* During the wait time, there are a variety of things you can do to prepare for construction. Enjoy this quiet time because once construction gets underway, things will be hopping.

You can access additional information that will help you become familiar with details and forms of standard agreements you may encounter in the "Critical Details to Include in Your Contracts with Architects and Contractors" report, found at the link below:

https://s3-us-west-1.amazonaws.com/stressfreeremodeling/Agreements.pdf

QUESTIONS: HOW TO COMMUNICATE SO THAT YOU GET WHAT YOU WANT

1.   Have you carefully defined your plan for your remodel?

2. What information have you found about your property from your city's Building Department, such as deed restrictions, former submittals for a project, or unusual easement requirements?

3. Do you have existing building drawings, property documents, etc.?

4. Have you established your budget and financing so that it matches your dream design?

5. What professional companies will you hire?

6. What is the type of architect and contractor you will look for?

7

HARD-WON LESSONS THAT YOU DON'T HAVE TO PAY FOR

Here are some important basics for a smoother and less stressful remodel that all homeowners wish they had known before starting their remodel:

- Research your property and products well.

- Understand the cost of building and your budget.

- Maintain a good communication flow with your construction team.

- Plan well.

- Be patient.

You may notice that this list is similar to the list of things to prepare before meeting with your architect. Research, communication, and planning are essential to maintain control of your team and your project. "If you are new to the remodeling process, you will have nothing against which to compare the progress of your own project, the performance of your players, or the time your process is taking. Every project is different, and even if you have gone through the process before there will be different challenges for each new situation," notes Jack Hawkins. The following stories of former clients and the lessons they learned the hard way will prove why these basics are critical to avoid calamities on your project, and hopefully spare you from experiencing them yourself.

RESEARCH YOUR PROPERTY, YOUR TEAM MEMBERS, AND YOUR PURCHASES

Make sure your plans comply with any restrictions on your property. You may find height restrictions or areas on which you may not build.

An acquaintance of mine once went to the expense of having plans drawn for a second-story addition without the guidance of an architect and couldn't get the plans approved when a height restriction was discovered. Time and money were wasted, resulting in having to move to another location with the dream of a second-story ocean view shattered.

Research each of your team members to be ensure they are reliable and trustworthy. Check out at least three references for each of your professionals. One of my clients hired a contractor based on someone's word without calling any of the contractor's former clients. After the contractor did not order and install sliding glass doors per the specifications, he started disappearing for days on end. The project ended up running way over budget and had many other issues. Later my clients found out from other sources that the contractor had caused havoc on several other projects, something they might have discovered if they had called references.

When you look for a surgeon to perform a serious operation on yourself or family member, you dig as deeply as you can to gather information about that surgeon, so you can have confidence, trust, and comfort about hiring them. Luckily your remodel isn't a life or death situation! But the same due diligence is recommended, nonetheless.

Ask your contractor to assist you with evaluating online and bargain appliance purchases, since they are up to date on products and may have professional sources not accessible by the general public. I hear about this from contractors such as Kevin Heldt who noted, "Clients try to save money by buying items such as refrigerators or heating equipment on online, but good warranties and other specifications that should be included with the product are often missing from these online purchases. The product that arrives may not have the optimal performance required or appropriate warranties. Your contractor's assistance and knowledge on these matters is well worth his fee."

You should feel confident that every product you incorporate, whether windows, hot water heaters, HVAC systems, and so on, serve your purpose, meet your budget, and have good warranties.

UNDERSTAND THE COST OF BUILDING YOUR PROJECT AND AVOID STICKER SHOCK

You've had the excitement of planning and designing your dreams. You've got your plans. And then you go to the bank and find out you're $100,000 short! Holding those plans in your hand, you know how great your life would be if only your home could be the vision you had on paper. What do you do now? Will you cry, wait to save up, beg-borrow-steal (please don't steal), or be disappointed with no project at all?

In this instance, there wasn't a realistic amount of research done on the project cost. Simple calculations using charts of typical building costs can give you a fairly accurate reality check. A basic formula is—

Remodeling Area square feet x Cost per square foot = Estimated project cost.

As mentioned before in Chapter 6.2, however, there are other expenses besides project cost that must be included, such as permits, in order to arrive at a realistic estimate of your total cost. Believe this number. Too many clients have a cost in their mind, and when the bids come in, they think they are all too high. Then they search for the cheapest contractor that can come close to their desired, but unrealistic, number. This inevitably results in disaster that ends up costing more than an original, reasonable bid.

Have a strong enough budget to build it right to last the first time, and don't skimp. Do as much as you can afford, especially with windows, insulation, doors, and heating systems. Such items as these will save you money in time.

MAINTAIN A GOOD COMMUNICATION FLOW

Establish a line of communication so when questions come up during construction, the contractor knows with whom to consult. Sometimes things aren't working as planned on the drawings, and a quick decision needs to be made. Communication is essential at decision points such as this one. If the plumber is installing a line to the kitchen sink but finds an air duct in the way and indiscriminately installs it two feet away from the specified location, here are the potential implications:

- The cabinets that have been ordered will not have the right configuration to accommodate the adjusted sink location.

- The granite countertop sink opening will not be in the proper location.

- The light fixture that was to be directly over the sink will not be in the proper location.

As you can see, one deviation from the plan without communicating about an issue can cause multiple new issues.

You can see the many ramifications of one decision. This is why a good line of communication between all your team members is important. If you are managing the project yourself in addition to your full-time job, and you are not available on-site, mistakes like this can occur. The plumber will be happy to relocate the plumbing to the proper location—for an additional fee of course—and the HVAC contractor will also have to relocate the vent to the proper location. This causes an increase in budget and time. A situation like this demonstrates the value of having a contractor and architect on site. They can recognize and handle issues like this before they create further complications.

Be sure to establish yourself as part of the decision-making because someone else may not resolve an issue the way you want. Whenever an important message or concern is sent to all the key players, you also need to be included. If there are any concerns or questions on your part, address them immediately to get them answered and resolved. Have the architect also involved in decisions because he or she understands the whole picture and impact a change can have on the entire project. The bottom line, says Jack Hawkins, "Direct and clear communication is the best."

You have heard of the old game of telephone where one person whispers a message into the ear of the next person who does the same to their next person, and so it goes around the circle. When the last person recites the message heard out loud, everyone has a good laugh at how garbled the message got. This is fun to laugh about in the game, but if it involves your remodel project, it is not a laughing matter. The lines of communication must be clear, open, and flowing.

Joy Spatz also emphasizes this point: "Communication regarding your project between you and the professionals of your team on and off the jobsite is critical. Also, as a couple supervising or working on your remodel together, communication between the two of you needs to be crystal clear. This is especially critical in the beginning of the project, so that everyone is on the same page about priorities, design, and budget. If you each have different agendas, there will be a conflict in the goal of the project. Confirming the project goals in each design phase is an important practice for continuing the success of the project."

PLAN WELL

Planning is another important element for a project. Issues to plan ahead for range from finances to decisions on what is going to be done, by whom, how, and when it will be completed.

It is important to make decisions on time when required by the architect or contractor. This is true whether it is a big decision such as finalizing your design, or a smaller one such as window selections. My colleague had a client who was not making decisions at the specified time. As a result, the client's windows were ordered late, so when the time came for them to be installed, the empty openings sat there on the exterior of the building in process, holding up the exterior and interior finishing. No one was very happy at that point. The construction crew had to stop work, which disrupted the contractor's schedule for the finish trades such as the drywall and exterior stuccowork, as well as delaying other projects.

Planning your project is important because there is much coordination and timing necessary for a critical sequence of work. Upsets in the flow of the project can case huge delays and costs. However, even though you have planned well, once construction begins, unexpected situations may be revealed. Knowing to expect minor disruptions and how to amend them will greatly ease your anxiety and keep the job moving along. One of my clients was recently held up with weather and concrete issues, who just said, "Oh well, we may as well enjoy the journey!" Great advice!

FIVE UNEXPECTED THINGS THAT CAN HAPPEN AND HOW TO FIX THEM

Even if you have the perfect plan for your remodel, surprises may be uncovered during the work. Regardless, do all you can to discover any of these potential culprits in advance to minimize surprises. Two easy precautions that will uncover potential problems are to have a professional home inspection performed, and also ask your contractor to do the most thorough inspection possible. These two inspections are similar to each other in their potential to locate problems, but the home inspection becomes an official document about the home stating any conditions found. While inspections can reveal obvious visible issues, they will not necessarily discover issues hidden behind walls, such as those below.

Five of the most common hidden issues that can cause potential delays and costs are as follows:

1. Mold, rot, insect infestation, or asbestos products.

2. Damaged or deteriorating foundations.

3. Plumbing that needs to be upgraded or replaced.

4. Electrical systems that need to be upgraded or replaced.

5. Missing structures that must be added.

1. Mold, Rot, Insect Infestation, or Asbestos

A home inspection can disclose situations of mold, rot, insect infestations, or asbestos if they are not hidden inside the walls. In the case of mold or infestation, the existing members that are affected will have to be removed and replaced. The inspection company or your contractor can do these repairs. Depending on the extent of the repairs, and in any case involving asbestos, a costly, specialized remediation process will be required.

2. Faulty Foundations

A home inspection can also disclose unstable foundations. Depending on the type, a faulty foundation will be reinforced or replaced, which will require digging out the adjacent earth to allow for the repairs.

If you are in an earthquake or wind zone, particular types of structure and bracing are required. Some of these structural requirements can be visibly detected, but others are behind drywall. Doing your early research with the building department will let you know if these systems are required so that you can include them in your budget.

3. Plumbing That Needs Replacing

If you have an older home, the existing plumbing may be outdated. If the old material has leaks or needs repairs, the entire system may have to be replaced, because old material often cannot be connected to new material. Old plumbing material is often not code compliant, either.

4. Electrical Systems That Need Upgrading

Electrical issues may not be visible since wiring systems are inside walls and ceilings. Electrical code requires grounded outlets, along with ground fault interrupter (GFI) outlets in bathrooms, kitchens, and outdoors. If you are remodeling these areas, your outlets will have to comply. In some jurisdictions where newer codes are used, all outlets must be GFIs. An older home may not have sufficient amperage in the circuit breakers to handle the load of the numerous electronic devices we use today. A circuit breaker like this will need to be upgraded.

On a project a few years ago, we removed an eight-foot ceiling that a previous remodeler had installed under the original stately ten-foot ceiling. There was a chandelier in the middle of the room. As the ceiling was removed, we discovered—to our horror—that the chandelier's electrical wire was extended from the original outlet in the ten-foot ceiling to the new, lower ceiling by splicing that wire to the new wire and simply taped together! It was amazing the house didn't burn down!

What I would like to know is, where was the inspector? Electrical codes exist for good reason, and this condition clearly violated them, creating a serious fire hazard in the space between the two ceilings. It is obvious the previous remodeler didn't get permits. As the homeowner you must be involved and monitor progress on your project. This is a pretty obvious situation to notice, but of course, you won't know everything to look for. Hence, this kind of situation illustrates good justification for having a (general) contractor on your job.

Costs for replacing or upgrading foundations, plumbing, electrical or structural elements can be significant, so it is important to understand if these issues will be involved and include them in your project's budget.

5. Missing Structures

Even if you have a set of existing drawings, inspections may reveal that the structure was not built as per the plans. Always review the existing plans to ensure they match what was built, and update them if necessary as you start your project. If there are no plans, you will need to do a survey to verify what is there. It is this survey on which your design team will base the new floor plan and structural plan. However, not every condition will be evident, even in a brand-new survey. In one instance, when widening a wall opening between a dining room and entry, we discovered a post was missing which should have supported a second story! With our new plan, we added the appropriate post and foundation.

If these items are not discovered before your remodel begins, the extra repairs will increase the construction time as well as increase the cost. Any of these conditions discovered during construction will require your contractor to issue you a change order. A change order is a document the contractor prepares and is approved by you stating the additional work and cost in order for the contractor to proceed with the work. Even if you are doing the work yourself, these surprises will add to the budget and lengthen the project schedule. This is an example of why you should include a contingency fund in your construction budget. A contingency fund is an amount set aside to cover unexpected items that must be corrected.

PLAN TO BE PATIENT AND ENJOY THE JOURNEY

You won't realize the time it takes to do a project. Clients always remark afterwards that they never realized the degree of detail and time that would be involved. As you have seen, every phase takes time, and possible delays are numerous and not always anyone's fault. The process cannot be rushed, so please have *patience, patience, patience.*

"It takes time to work out a good design, and a good design is easily the most important part of a project, on which all the rest of the project depends," agree both Bill Fisher and Jack Hawkins. "Each decision you make will usually require five other decisions before you can arrive at that one. Take time to consider and understand those decisions."

It takes the architect a great deal of coordination, research, and physical time to prepare your drawings, so be mindful and appreciate they are doing their best to be productive in a timely manner. *Patience.*

The permitting process may take weeks or months, depending where you are located. *Patience.*

The construction will go quickly in the beginning, as you see your vision come into being, but the finishing will seem to drag on forever. *Patience, patience, patience.*

You will get there.

QUESTIONS: FIVE HARD-WON LESSONS THAT YOU DON'T HAVE TO PAY FOR

1. Do your plans comply with any restrictions imposed on your property?

2. When will you schedule a home inspection?

3. Do all of your professionals' references check out?

4. Have you refined the estimated cost of your project, and are you comfortable with the amount?

5. Do you feel you can make decisions in a timely manner throughout the project?

6. What products and finishes will you research for your project?

7. What strategy will you use to help keep your patience throughout the project?

8

FIVE STEPS TO HOME REMODEL SUCCESS

Whether you are doing a small, $9,000, DIY kitchen remodel project over two months, or you are doing a major, $290,000 remodel that will take nine months or more to complete, the design and the implementation processes will be the same, even though the dollars and time will vary.

The steps listed below will prepare you for your remodeling process whether you are doing it yourself or collaborating with an architect.

1. Envision and evaluate

2. Research

3. Establish budget and finances

4. Initiate your plans and/or hire your team

5. Plan the details to a T

This process can seem overwhelming, but if you break it down step-by-step, have the right information, know what to expect, identify what you need, and get professional guidance, the process will go smoothly from phase to phase, and you will achieve amazing results.

1. ENVISION AND EVALUATE

Envision what your end result will be. Collect images of what you want your dream remodel to look like. Images are a good way to communicate what you have in mind to your architect and contractor(s). They can describe style, detail, and even the kinds of materials that appeal to you. Viewing your selected images will help the architect and contractor begin to estimate the remodel cost.

Evaluate your family's lifestyle, what your present home is lacking, and what options will make it wonderful. Answer questions such as—

- What do you want it to look like?
- What are the improvements you want to make?
- What additions to your home do you want to make?
- How will you use your new space?
- How will it make you feel?

2. RESEARCH

Doing research in the early stages of your planning is invaluable. Research your property to discover any limitations or deed restrictions on your lot before you begin to plan. This will prevent you from designing a project that has a larger scope than is allowed or creating a plan to build in a particular area that is not allowed. You may also find other information to help you strategize through the planning process and learn whether your jurisdiction requires additional approval processes.

Covenants, conditions, and restrictions (CCRs) are rules and limitations on your home and property enforced by a Homeowner's Association. If you are in a community that enforces CCRs, investigate and understand their criteria. Many communities have limits on design, style, building materials, and exterior colors.

3. ESTABLISH YOUR FINANCES

Knowing what you can spend on your remodel and clarifying your plan and scope of work go hand-in-hand. As you gather your information in the first step of envisioning and evaluating, also research actual building costs for ideas like yours in your local area to keep your vision and finances in balance. Keep in mind that there are numerous fees to include in your preliminary estimated budget and financing, many of which aren't obvious.

Know how much you have to invest in your project and consider whether you should compromise or wait, so you can include all your desires. This is a very important exercise to do so that time, money, and emotion are not misspent on a plan your finances cannot support.

Mentioning budget yet again may seem redundant, but the budget is a "biggie." Without a good understanding of what your costs and budget are up front, you can experience great emotional and financial distress later on. If you run into unexpected expenses, or decide to increase the scope of your project, you want the remodel to move forward without hesitation and without you going bankrupt.

When considering how much you want to invest, you can ask a realtor to help you compare your home to the value of similar homes in your neighborhood. Typically, you don't want to invest an amount that raises the value of your home significantly higher than the surrounding homes.

4. INITIATE: TAKE ACTION ON YOUR PLANS AND/OR HIRE YOUR TEAM

If you are doing a small project yourself, then you will be ready to take action on your plan after completing the three steps suggested above.

This is the time to get your architect on board to translate and incorporate your ideas, wants, and needs into a plan that meets your requirements. Take advantage of their creativity and do not rush through the design phase. This is a very important aspect of the project, where you develop rapport and understanding with the architect. It is when the most amazing design magic happens.

Next, secure your general contractor to assist you with assessing costs, and in some cases construction methods, as the project develops. Keeping tabs on the budget as each phase progresses gives you the opportunity to adjust early, rather than trying to recover from sticker shock later or eliminating elements that have already become dear to you.

Managing the construction phase is a daily activity. The architect may not be on site every day. If you do not have a general contractor on your team, take the initiative to be involved to ensure that the plans are being built as per the intent of the drawings. If you are living in your home during construction, you can easily monitor the progress. Once you see your ideas being built, they may not meet your expectations. Sometimes the vision is different on paper than in reality, or some great design opportunity presents itself. Revisions to your plans can be made for such reasons; however, you will need to notify the architect and contractor as soon as possible.

5. PLAN THE DETAILS TO A T

Planning is one of the most important elements of a remodel on multiple levels. The first three steps are part of the planning sequence; much of the planning involves allowing for time factors and various building tasks that must occur in a particular sequence.

The following are some of the numerous factors to consider when estimating how much time to allow for your project:

- Allow the time to develop your new design ideas, both before you meet with your architect, and also with him or her after you have shared your initial ideas.

- Allow time for the design process with your architect. The design phase of a project is an extremely important phase, one on which the whole project rests.

- Allow time for the architect and other consultants to do their work for you. Every project varies in the degree of size and complexity. Your architect can give you an estimate for the amount of time it will take to complete their work.

- When working with a contractor and architect, plan your decision-making process to be efficient and swift.

- Allow time for the permitting process. The timeline to acquire necessary permits can vary depending on your location. In a busy urban area where there is a lot of building activity, it may require months. In a smaller community where there is not much building activity and less stringent and rigorous regulatory requirements, the permitting process should move along much more quickly. To get an idea of the timelines in your area, contact your local building and safety department. Also, your architect and contractor should have a sense of your local area's permit review process based on their most recent experiences.

- Allow time for construction and completion. Your contractor will be able to estimate the length of construction time upon reviewing the architectural plans.

- Allow time for inspections. Various inspections will be planned throughout the construction phase to assure building methods and codes are met. The final inspection and the issue of the Certificate of Occupancy, a certificate issued by the Building Department, legally finalizes your project and allows you to reside in your new home.

The last stretch will require patience since, at this point, you will want it to be over! Use that time to plan what you will need to settle in after your move-in date. And don't forget to plan your celebration!

Throughout your remodel, there will be many processes taking place at once, some of which you will not be part of, and there may be periods when you don't hear of much progress. Your hardest task at these times will be to have patience every step of the way.

If you are organizing the project yourself, the planning items will be the same, only you will be responsible for the entire project's planning and scheduling.

QUESTIONS: 5 STEPS TO HOME REMODEL SUCCESS

1. Do you have the final vision of how your new home will look?

2. Are there any clues in your property documents that can help strategize the design and approvals?

3. Is your budget and financing finalized?

4. Are you happy with the design professionals you hired?

5. Who will be on your guest list for your new home celebration?

9

WRAP UP

My hope for you is that, after reading this book, you feel more at ease with what the remodeling process is about and that after taking action on the suggested steps for your project, you will have the confidence to undertake your plan.

I wish you an enjoyable remodeling experience and a beautiful new home to enjoy for years to come!

If you would like more detailed support for your remodeling process, I offer *The Ultimate Stress-Free Home Remodeling Blueprint*, a five-module online video program that is accessible at your convenience. It will—

- Give you confidence and control of your remodel project.

- Give you tools to stay on budget and time.

- Help you relax, knowing what to expect.

Group coaching calls are also available. More information can be found at the link below:

https://stressfreeremodeling.com/program

And don't forget to join our *Stress-Free Remodeling Exchange* on Facebook where I provide current design and building trends and where homeowners like you can share their ideas, experiences, resources, and fun! You can find us on Facebook at the link below:

https://www.facebook.com/groups/1595182977178750

Also, you can subscribe to my *Stress-Free Remodeling Podcast* where I introduce experts from various related building industries who share their expertise, experiences, and unique perspectives about all aspects of remodeling. Find the podcast on iTunes at the following link:

https://itunes.apple.com/us/podcast/stress-free-remodeling/id1438998766?mt=2

Or if you are not an iTunes user:
http://stressfreeremodeling.libsyn.com/

A toast to your new dream home!
Happy remodeling!

ABOUT THE AUTHOR

Practically born on a job site, Emma Auriemma-McKay was destined to be an architect. Drawing fantasy floor plans at the age of 12, her favorite floor plan back then was a hexagonal "donut" design that had a courtyard in the center of the home. But it wasn't until she was introduced to her biggest inspiration and hero in a high school art class, Leonardo Da Vinci, that she started to experiment with her ideas. She was fascinated by his vast abilities and knew she wanted to be like him.

Recognizing that her passions paralleled Da Vinci's led her to become a licensed architect and interior designer, an award-winning painter, and the creator of the online program *The Ultimate Stress-Free Home Remodeling Blueprint* that guides homeowners through their home remodeling projects.

Emma's mission is to make the world a more beautiful and better functioning place for everyone. Growing up in New Jersey, she couldn't wait to see the world! At 18, she set off to satisfy her wanderlust. After graduating from the Rhode Island School of Design, she travelled throughout Europe, Asia, Africa, and the United States. She fell in love with each country's culture, architecture, food, and arts. Her favorite trips were to Italy where she ate lots of pizza, pasta, and gelato and savored her rich Italian heritage. These travels have had a great influence on her life and her work.

As an architect, Emma started off working with international firms in New York, Los Angeles, and London where she was involved in many high-rise commercial structures, residential developments, and luxury hotels such as the Mandalay Bay and Four Seasons, Las Vegas, and the Hilton Hawaiian Village, Honolulu. She then settled in California where she began her own architectural practice, focusing on residential projects and remodels of her own.

Emma believes it's important to give back to her community. She has offered up her design, art, and culinary talents to the various organizations to which she belongs.

Now residing in the foothills of the Sierra Nevada, Emma, her husband, and their adopted dog Pepper love being surrounded by the dramatic landscape and epic seasons of Reno, Nevada. When she's not in the office or working with the community, you can find Emma drawing, painting, hiking, traveling, and dancing.

Made in the USA
San Bernardino, CA
22 July 2019